GARDEN GUIDES

PATIOS, POTS & WINDOW BOXES

GARDEN GUIDES

PATIOS, POTS & WINDOW BOXES

SUE AND ROGER NORMAN

Illustrations by
ELAINE FRANKS

CHARTWELL
BOOKS, INC.

Published by Chartwell Books
a division of Book Sales, Inc.
114 Northfield Avenue
Edison, NJ 08837

This edition produced for sale
in the U.S.A., its territories
and dependencies only.

ISBN 0-7858-0528-1

Produced by Robert Ditchfield Ltd

Printed and bound in Italy

CONTENTS

Poisonous Plants

In recent years, concern has been voiced about poisonous plants or plants which can cause allergic reactions if touched. The fact is that many plants are poisonous, some in a particular part, others in all their parts. For the sake of safety, it is always, without exception, essential to assume that no part of a plant should be eaten unless it is known, without any doubt whatsoever, that the plant or its part is edible and that it cannot provoke an allergic reaction in the individual person who samples it. It must also be remembered that some plants can cause severe dermatitis, blistering or an allergic reaction if touched, in some individuals and not in others. It is the responsibility of the individual to take all the above into account.

How to Use This Book

Where appropriate, approximate measurements of a plant's height have been given, and also the spread where this is significant, in both metric and imperial measures. The height is the first measurement, as for example 1.2m × 60cm/4 × 2ft. However, both height and spread vary so greatly from garden to garden since they depend on soil, climate and position, that these measurements are offered as guides only. This is especially true of trees and shrubs where ultimate growth can be unpredictable.

The following symbols are also used throughout the book:

❍ = thrives best or only in full sun
◐ = thrives best or only in part-shade
● = succeeds in full shade
E = evergreen

Where no sun symbol and no reference to sun or shade is made in the text, it can be assumed that the plant tolerates sun or light shade.

Plant Names

For ease of reference this book gives the botanical name under which a plant is most widely listed for the gardener. These names are sometimes changed and in such cases the new name has been included. Common names are given wherever they are in frequent use.

Patios, Pots and Window Boxes

A patio or paved area next to your house can be a joy for ever, if you get it right. The site will usually dictate the materials to be used and plants that will grow best.

Away from the house, paved or terraced areas give much more freedom in the choice of plants and construction materials.

Think carefully how you want to use the area. If you want a barbecue, then more of your patio will need to provide a level, uncluttered space for tables and chairs. If it is to be used by children, then safe surfaces and few vulnerable pots will be required. If plants are to be the main interest, then the aspect of the site will dictate what will grow best.

You must consider your planting plans at the design stage. The range of choices is enormous. Crevice planting? Borders? Raised beds? Pots and containers? Water feature? Climbers?

Be careful to choose materials which blend or contrast effectively with the surroundings and which are practical. Do not use gravel where children run, or where it will be walked into the house, and beware of smooth surfaces in shaded areas; they can be very slippery in winter.

Be sure to use adequate foundations and that the area drains properly.

Planting Patios and Terraces

How you plant your paved area will depend a lot on how much time you have available to look after it. It is no use developing a mass planting scheme in pots and containers for summer colour on a hot patio if you are not going to be there to water it twice a day in high summer, although there are automatic watering systems which would help.

Planting in containers has the enormous advantage of flexibility. You can have different schemes throughout the year and can grow plants that would not grow in your garden soil.

Beds offer easier growing conditions – larger root runs and less demanding watering – but are less flexible. Raised beds offer the added dimension of height and can be filled with the soil of your choice.

Many plants like to grow in the gaps between paving. This environment gives a cool root run which does not dry out quickly and, if the gaps are filled with gravel, this ensures a dry area round the neck of the plant, which is much appreciated by many alpines. Areas which are heavily walked on require tougher, shorter plants.

This well-planted patio has room for a table and chairs beneath a pergola which provides shade and overhead colour from plants. It is sturdy enough to support hanging baskets.

(Left) A flight of steps shows off potted plants to advantage as it grades their heights. Here alyssum, violas, pansies, fuchsia and lobelia benefit from the shelter of the wall.

(Opposite left) A large tender *Aeonium arboreum* in a pot is put outside in summer. It leads the eye to Ali Baba jars planted with herbs on the steps.

Choosing Pots and Containers

When choosing pots and containers it is important to consider how they will look in their surroundings and what plants you will put in them. Tall plants, especially in windy places, need broad-based containers. Alpines look best in sinks, troughs or shallow pans. Trailing plants need taller containers, such as chimney pots.

The range of pots and containers available to gardeners is enormous, from antique stone or lead cisterns to plastic pots. For those with a creative streak, almost anything can be adapted, provided it has drainage holes. If they are to be used outside in cold winter areas, containers must be frost resistant. Also, porous containers left outside in frosty conditions should be raised clear of solid surfaces on pieces of slate, or special ornamental feet.

Planting

Almost any plant can be grown in a container: even forest trees can be grown as Bonsai subjects. It is important to strike the right balance between size of plant, size of pot, compost strength and plant vigour. It is better to

repot a plant frequently than to put a small plant straight into a large container.

Loam-based composts are the easiest to use for plants in pots and containers; they hold moisture and fertilizers better than other composts. Possible exceptions to this are composts for hanging baskets and window boxes, where weight is an important consideration.

It is necessary to use an ericaceous compost for rhododendrons, azaleas, heathers and other lime-hating plants.

Most plants need feeding and this can be achieved by adding fertilizers to the compost

A row of trimmed box in pots gives the effect of a neat hedge.

(Above) An old lead cistern with pelargoniums and a purple cotinus.

(Left) A tiny terrace with scented lilies beside the seat.

and by liquid feeding when watering. Annuals and soft perennials planted closely to flower over a long period need a strong compost and frequent liquid feeds. Trees and shrubs need a compost with relatively large amounts of slow release fertilizer, liquid feeding and annual repotting. They can be maintained in their final containers for some years by removing annually in spring as much compost as possible, without too much root disturbance, and replacing with fresh compost containing controlled-release fertilizer. Trees and shrubs will also need pruning to give them shape and to improve flowering.

Plants in containers tend to dry out very quickly and need frequent watering. During hot summer periods, hanging baskets and some pots will need watering twice a day. Equipment can be used to help with watering. Additives are also available which are designed to retain water in the compost and to aid rewetting dried-out composts.

(Above) Red flowers are set off by foliage in this swagged pot under a hood.

(Right) A lovely and slightly tender *Abutilon megapotamicum*.

Most annuals and soft perennials need dead-heading regularly to keep them flowering throughout the season.

SITING

Pots and containers can be used in a variety of ways from the dramatic to the utilitarian. A group of herb-filled pots are an asset by the kitchen door or in a window box. Succulents and pelargoniums give a sunny corner a Mediterranean look, and a group of scented plants, either similar or contrasting, can be placed by a seat or along a narrow path. Pots can be used to disguise, or distract the eye from, unattractive features. Pots of lilies can be plunged in borders to fill gaps and enhance colour schemes. A large container can be used to dramatic effect as a focal point or as the centre piece in a formal border. An interesting container can be very effective even when unplanted. Containers can give emphasis to doors, gates, arches and steps.

1. Planting a Patio

A paved area can create a very special climate for a range of plants you cannot grow elsewhere.

PAVING PLANTS

At the design stage specify lots of gaps for plants, but leave some room for people!

Small, self-seeding plants, like *Erinus alpinus* (Fairy foxglove) and *Inopsidium acaule* (Violet cress) thrive in paving cracks.

The green leaves, pinkish stems and white flowers of this stonecrop make a good combination. The full name of this plant is ***Sedum album*** ssp. ***teretifolium*** var. ***murale*** ❍, 7.5 × 45cm/3in × 1½ft.

PLANTS IN THE GAPS BETWEEN PAVING soften the edges and add interest to your patio. Take care to leave clear walking areas. Thymes, creeping mints and chamomile may be planted on the edges of routes, as they tolerate bruising and are aromatic, whereas sempervivums are easily broken and do better in a sunny corner, out of the way of people's feet.

There are many varieties of **sempervivum** (**houseleeks**), all of them decorative, even heraldic in shape with their evergreen rosettes and starry flowers in summer. After flowering, the individual rosette dies, but surrounding offsets continue. ❍, E, 10cm/4in by indefinite spread.

Paving Plants

DIANTHUS – PINKS – are amongst the prettiest small midsummer flowers and will grow well with their heads in the sun and their roots in the cool, moist conditions under the paving. Unless you are strictly a summer gardener you will want some interest at other seasons, such as spring bulbs, dwarf conifers and saxifrages which flower in spring and have attractive all-year foliage.

Campanula garganica
Beautiful, dwarf perennial with starry flowers ideally suited to a paving crevice, summer to autumn.
15 × 45cm/6in × 1½ft

Use a gravel that blends with your paving to cover the soil.

Endeavour to keep the gravel just below the paving level to minimize its spread by feet.

Old-fashioned pinks are very fragrant but have only one main flush of flowers. Modern varieties will flower recurrently if dead-headed regularly.

PAVING PLANTS

WHEN BUYING PLANTS to put between your paving you need to consider the size of the gap available. Small, young plants tend to establish more easily than larger, older ones. Whatever their size, ensure that they have sufficient soil for their roots to develop.

Campanula hallii Little white bells over good green foliage. 5 × 60cm/2in × 2ft

Androsace lanuginosa Clusters of blush or lilac-pink flowers mass the trailing mat of silky leaves. ❍, 5 × 30cm/2in × 1ft

Scilla sibirica Easy spring bulb, blooming year after year, needing little attention. ◐, 10–15cm/4–6in tall

Campanula cochleariifolia var. ***pallida* 'Miranda'** One of the very best with many slate-blue flowers. 5 × 60cm/2in × 2ft

Troughs combine well with paved areas, adding height and more planting opportunities. Pots, or ornaments, can be used to emphasize pathways and to lead the eye to the rest of the garden.

◆ *Almost fill the crevice with gravel round the neck of the plant, to conserve moisture and ease weeding.*

PAVING PLANTS

***Erinus alpinus* (Fairy foxglove)** For walls and crevices. Flowers are various pinks and white.
❍, E, 2.5–5cm/1–2in tall

Phlox subulata Evergreen mat. Spring-flowering. Many different forms, any colour except yellow. ❍, E, 10 × 30–60cm/4in × 1–2ft

Phuopsis stylosa Forms a shaggy bright green mat massed with pink flowers all summer.
❍, 30 × 45cm/1 × 1½ft

***Acaena* 'Blue Haze'** Spreading mats of steel-blue leaflets and sticky dark red burr heads in summer.
E, 10 × 60cm/4in × 2ft

Cotoneaster congestus Small white flowers in spring, large red berries.
E, mat-forming

***Trifolium repens* 'Purpurascens'** Purple-leaved form of the common clover. ❍, mat-forming

Ajuga reptans There are many forms with different coloured leaves.
15 × 45cm/6in × 1½ft

***Sedum spurium* 'Dragon's Blood'** A showy stonecrop. Mat-forming. ❍, semi-E, 10 × 45cm/4in × 1½ft

◆ *Late flowering sedums such as this attract butterflies.*

Evergreens *and* Small Trees

Evergreens and small trees provide a long term shape to a patio, giving a quiet background to spring, summer colour and some interest in the winter. Unless planted in containers, they are fairly permanent features and should be chosen with care.

Magnolia stellata One of the best dwarf shrubby trees. Flowers, white, scented, mid-spring. 2.4 × 2.4m/8 × 8ft

***Thuja occidentalis* 'Rheingold'** Conifers come in many different forms and shapes. Some, like *Thuja orientalis* 'Rosedalis', change colour with the seasons, green in spring, purple in winter. E, 1m × 60cm/3 × 2ft

◆ *Check that the conifer you choose is dwarf.*

***Buxus sempervirens* (Box)** This tough evergreen shrub can be used for topiary and has many variegated forms. E, 2.7 × 2.7m/9 × 9ft

◆ *Here the box has been trimmed to form balls in tubs.*

EVERGREENS *and* SMALL TREES

***Choisya ternata* (Mexican orange blossom)** Appreciates a sheltered sunny position. Flowers, white, mainly in spring. The glossy leaves are aromatic when crushed. E, 2 × 2.4m/6 × 8ft

◆ *'Aztec Pearl' and 'Sundance' are attractive varieties of choisya.*

***Garrya elliptica* (Tassel bush)** A quick-growing, bushy shrub with long 20cm/8in catkins in winter. Does well on a shady wall. Popular with flower arrangers.
E, 4 × 3m/12 × 10ft

EVERGREENS *and* SMALL TREES

For permanent plantings choose plants which are hardy in your area.

Before planting, place the plants in position and check from various angles that they are in the best positions.

WHEN SPACE IS RESTRICTED, permanent larger plants must be chosen with care to provide more than one season of interest. Take into account a combination of foliage, flower, fruit, autumn colour and bark.

Cotoneaster White flowers and colourful fruits. Cotoneasters come in many shapes and sizes from prostrate to weeping standards.

***Camellia* 'Frau Minna Seidel'** ('Otome' 'Pink Perfection') Early flowers. Shelter from early morning sun.
◐, E, 2 × 2m/6 × 6ft

***Cistus* 'Elma'** Papery flowers open in the morning and fall in the evening, more appearing each day in summer.
❍, E, 1.2 × 1.2m/4 × 4ft

Daphne tangutica Slow growing, easy. Flowers in early summer. Red berries.
E, 1 × 1 m/3 × 3 ft

◆ *Many daphnes are renowned for the scent of their flowers.*

Ballota pseudodictamnus A much branched shrub, with soft foliage and bobble 'flowers' in summer.
E, 45 × 60cm/1½ × 2ft

Fabiana imbricata violacea Heathlike appearance when young, spreading with age. Prefers a light soil.
◐, E, 2.2 × 2m/7 × 6ft

Evergreens *and* Small Trees

***Cytisus praecox* 'Allgold'** A bushy broom with arching branches, grey-green leaves and rich yellow flowers in spring. ❍, 1.5 × 2m/5 × 6ft

***Picea glauca* 'Albertiana Conica'** Slowly grows into a dense cone with fine, grass green foliage. E, 1m × 45cm/ 3 × 1½ft in ten years

***Artemisia* 'Powis Castle'** Aromatic silver filigree foliage contrasts with bright summer colours. E, 60 × 60cm/2 × 2ft

Hypericum olympicum Small shrub with grey-green leaves and golden yellow flowers in summer. ❍, 30 × 30cm/1 × 1ft

***Lonicera nitida* 'Baggesen's Gold'** Small-leaved evergreen. Keeps its colour well in winter. ❍, 1.5 × 2m/5 × 6ft

Laurus nobilis (Sweet bay) Often trimmed to make a topiary ball. Needs shelter. ❍, E, 6 × 6m/20 × 20ft

Erica arborea alpina Compact tree heath with plumes of tiny white flower bells in winter/spring. E, 1.2m/4ft height and spread

***Malus × moerlandsii* 'Profusion'** The modern varieties of crab apple have attractive features in most seasons with flowers, fruit and autumn leaf colour. 6 × 4m/20 × 13ft

PLANTS *for a* HOT TERRACE

Gazania makes a super display in summer sun with its bright colours and silver leaves. Needs protection from frost but can be overwintered as cuttings.

There are many helianthemums and pinks from which to choose. Propagate by cuttings after flowering.

Many plants will have a prolonged flowering season if dead-headed regularly, especially helianthemums and mesembryanthemums.

THE HOT TERRACE is ideal, providing the drainage is good, for Mediterranean plants and sun lovers. Plants with leaves that are woolly, waxy, silver or narrow and small tolerate drought most readily, but should never be allowed to dry out.

***Armeria maritima* (Thrift)** Forms a neat hump, enjoying sun and wind. Flowers can be white, pink or red. 7.5 × 15cm/3 × 6in

Convolvulus cneorum Glistening silver-green leaves, flowering all summer. Not fully hardy. E, 60 × 60cm/2 × 2ft

***Dianthus* 'Waithman's Beauty'** A neat, ground-hugging pink, appreciating good drainage and lime in the soil. E, 10 × 15cm/ 4 × 6in

***Linum narbonense* 'Heavenly Blue'** A hardy plant with grey-green leaves and abundant flowers. 40 × 30cm/16 × 12in

Helianthemum (Rock rose) Makes mounds of evergreen foliage topped with bright flowers. E, 15 × 60cm/6in × 2ft

Mesembryanthemum (Livingstone daisy) Succulent leaves. Bright flowers open in sun. 15 × 15cm/6 × 6in

Triteleia laxa Californian bulb. Loose, many-headed blue-purple flowers in summer. Best near a warm wall. 60cm/2ft

PLANTS *for a* HOT TERRACE

EVEN THOUGH YOUR PLANTS ARE DROUGHT-TOLERANT they will need water, especially until they are established. It is better to soak the plants thoroughly once a week than to water a little each day, which encourages surface-rooting.

Carpenteria californica Bushy shrub with glossy leaves. Single anemone-shaped flowers. Sunny wall. E, 3 × 2m/10 × 6ft

Hibiscus Beautiful tropical-looking blooms and shiny green leaves. Suffers bud-drop if too dry at the roots. 2 × 1.2m/6 × 4ft

Genista lydia Arching or prostrate grey-green branches, linear leaves and bright yellow flowers. 75cm × 2m/2½ × 6ft

Buddleja alternifolia Pretty bush with narrow pale leaves on arching stems. Good as a standard. 3.5 × 4.5m/12 × 15ft

***Cordyline australis* 'Atropurpurea'** Slow-growing tender plant. E, 7.5 × 2.4m/25 × 8ft

◆ *This New Zealand cabbage palm bears plumes of fragrant flowers when 8–10 years old.*

PLANTS *for a* HOT TERRACE

COLOUR IS VERY MUCH A MATTER OF INDIVIDUAL TASTE, but, if you fancy a change from red and shocking pink, this beautiful cistus illustrated opposite in dazzling white with the blue of the ceanothus, set off by the silver and grey foliage plants, produces a bright but cooler effect.

***Rosmarinus officinalis* (Rosemary)** Evergreen, aromatic shrub with attractive spring flowers usually in shades of blue, but white and pink varieties are available, as are prostrate and upright forms.

Ceanothus impressus A vigorous evergreen shrub with deep green glossy leaves and many clusters of flowers in early spring. Californian 'lilacs' are not the hardiest of shrubs, but grow so well on a wall that they are worth risking. E, 3 × 3m/10 × 10ft

These shrubs prefer poorer soils and, if overfed, are more susceptible to frost damage.

Prune evergreen ceanothus, if required, after flowering; and deciduous, autumn-flowering ones, hard as they come into growth.

***Lavandula* (Lavender)** An indispensable fragrant shrub that is the source of lavender oil. There are many types, some with white or pink flowers, others with leaves that vary from apple green to silver. Attractive to bees and butterflies. E, 30cm–1.2m/1–4ft height and spread

PLANTS *for* *a* SHADY TERRACE

***Camellia* 'Inspiration'**
Camellias thrive best in light, acid soils enriched with leaf mould to help retain moisture. They prefer dappled shade, or a cool wall. ◐, E, 3 × 2m/ 10 × 6ft

Rhododendrons come in all shapes and sizes. Flower colours are from near blue to red, pink, white and yellow. Some are scented.

Use spring bulbs such as bluebells, wood anemones and dog's tooth violets to fill gaps.

The variegated forms of *Vinca minor* maintain their foliage colour throughout the year.

IN A SHADY POSITION foliage assumes great importance, as woodland plants tend to be less floriferous and brightly coloured than sun lovers. Plants with large lush leaves that wilt and scorch in sun and wind will thrive in moist shade. Colour is an important consideration. White and gold are the most dramatic colours in shade. Variegated foliage will provide pools of light against green backgrounds.

***Aucuba japonica* 'Variegata'**
Few shrubs tolerate shade as well as aucubas. A variegated form will brighten any dark corner. E, 3 × 2 m/10 × 6 ft

***Rhododendron* 'Praecox'**
Rosy mauve flowers early in the year; best protected from frost by overhead tree canopy. All rhododendrons need acid soil. ◐, E, 1.2–2 × 1.2–2m/4–6 × 4–6ft

◆ *Winter aconites,* Eranthis hyemalis, *are very effective planted around rhododendrons.*

Hydrangeas are excellent shrubs for mid and late summer in light shade and moisture retentive soils. The dying flower heads turn an attractive colour and should not be pruned away until growth starts in the spring. Flower colour can be affected by the acidity/alkalinity of the soil.

***Hydrangea* serrata 'Grayswood'** Blue fertile flowers surrounded by large white ray florets which mature to crimson. A beautiful hybrid of lax habit, needing light shade. 1.2 × 1.2m/4 × 4ft

PLANTS *for a* SHADY TERRACE

Cotoneaster horizontalis Deciduous shrub with herringbone branches. Pink flowers followed by red berries. 60cm × 2m/ 2 × 6ft, taller against a wall

***Hedera helix* 'Parsley Crested'** Attractive ivy which will cling to most surfaces and eventually cover a large area, in sun or shade.

Parthenocissus henryana Self-clinging climber. Variegated leaves, best in shade, brilliant red in autumn. 10m/30ft height

Fatsia japonica This is grown for its handsome evergreen foliage and dramatic white flowers in autumn. 3 × 3m/10 × 10ft

Skimmia japonica Fragrant flowers in spring followed by red berries (male and female plants required). E, 1.2 × 2m/4 × 6ft

Pernettya (Gaultheria) mucronata Lime-hating. Berries in autumn, colour dependent on variety. E, 1.2m × 60cm/4 × 2ft

***Mahonia aquifolium* (Oregon grape)** Suckering shrub, fragrant yellow flowers in spring, blue-black berries. E, 1.2 × 2m/4 × 6ft

***Convallaria majalis* (Lily of the valley)** Arching stems carry sweet smelling flowers in early spring. 15 × 60cm/6in × 2ft

Bergenia cordifolia A tough plant with shiny, leathery leaves. Pink early-spring flowers. E, 30 × 60cm/ 1 × 2ft

***Asplenium scolopendrium* (Hart's tongue fern)** for walls. Adiantum ferns for damp; polystichums for dry shade.

Plants *for* a Shady Terrace

Few plants grow well in complete shade. Deciduous trees and shrubs allow more light in winter, providing better conditions for spring bulbs and herbaceous plants, such as hellebores and pulsatillas, which flower early in the year.

Polygonatum* × *hybridum Solomon's seal with attractive arching stems and white flowers in early summer. 1m × 30cm/3 × 1ft

Cyclamen hederifolium Flowers from late summer into winter. The marbled leaves persist until spring. 7.5 × 30cm/3in × 1ft

Primula vulgaris There are very many double forms of the primrose. 15 × 30cm/6in × 1ft

Divide double primroses when they start to get congested, about every three years.

Sawfly larvae will eat polygonatum leaves in midsummer. Spray insecticide or pick them off.

Bedding

Shady areas tend to lack brightness, and bedding plants and bulbs will supply more colour. Use daffodils, winter aconites and hyacinths for spring, impatiens (*right*) for summer and, later, winter pansies.

◆ Digitalis purpurea *(foxgloves) will brighten dark areas. They are biennials, flowering in their second year.*

A PERGOLA ADDS AN EXTRA DIMENSION to your terrace. It provides shade in summer and is a great way to display climbers. To grow well the plants will need to be placed in a border or in 60cm/2ft planting holes. It may help the more delicate climbers to put wires or netting on the posts for extra support. When combining climbers on a pergola, check that pruning regimes are compatible.

CLIMBERS *for* PERGOLAS

***Clematis* 'Gipsy Queen'** A vigorous grower with a three-month flowering season. The flowers are 15cm/6in in diameter and combine well with a pink rose. 3.5–6m/12–20ft

◆ *Clematis prefer cool root runs, so plant on the shady side of the post.*

Wisteria The classic spring flower for a pergola, but it needs to be trained and pruned. Halve and tie in the new growth in summer. In winter halve the extension shoots again and prune side shoots to three buds.

Rosa **'Madame Grégoire Staechelin'** A vigorous climber with a profusion of double, scented flowers in early summer. Prefers some shade. 3.5–6m/12–20ft

◆ *This rose makes an ideal support for a late-flowering clematis.*

2. Pots and Hanging Baskets

Pots and containers have three great virtues: they can be moved anywhere, you can give plants the conditions they need and you can easily change them.

Choosing Pots

Containers come in all shapes and sizes. Large pots are easier to maintain as they do not dry out as quickly as small ones. All pots must have drainage holes. Terracotta is the traditional material for ornamental pots, but make sure that your pot will withstand frost if it is left outside in winter.

Choosing Pots

Strawberry Pot
Use a strong compost and take care to leave sufficient room to water without washing the soil away.

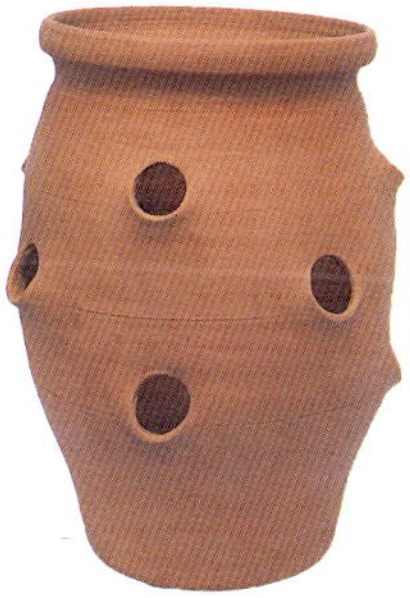

Herb Pot
Watering is a problem with this type of container. A pipe with holes in it, placed centrally, will help.

Plastic Pot
These come in many shapes and sizes, are relatively cheap and easy to handle. They are not porous and therefore do not dry out as quickly as terracotta.

Wall Pot
Be sure the fixings are strong enough for the combined weight of pot, wet compost and plants.

Reconstituted Stone
These can be aged with diluted cow manure or liquid fertilizer, to encourage algae.

Wooden tubs and barrels make good containers but may need some maintenance to prevent rotting.

Concrete containers are cheap but very heavy – they do not blow over easily!

Glazed Pot And Saucer
In wet weather, check that the saucer is not full of water.

SITING CONTAINERS

Colour co-ordinated pots. Many different plants grouped together can look something of a hotch-potch but care with the choice of shape and colour makes this an attractive feature.

◆ *Unity is added to the group by using pots of the same material.*

Phormium* (New Zealand flax) and *Aruncus dioicus This shows how effective a pot can be when temporarily placed by a border with the plants complementing each other. The bronze form of phormium shows up well against the cream background.

Aeonium in a pot 'playing a role' in a gravel bed. Plants normally confined to the greenhouse can be used in summer to give a dramatic impact in the garden.

◆ *Many house and greenhouse plants appreciate a summer out of doors.*

SITING CONTAINERS

CONTAINERS CAN ENLIVEN DULL CORNERS, fill gaps in borders, hide manhole covers, distract the eye from ugly buildings, make herb gardens by the kitchen door or hold scented plants near a seat. They are movable gardens and are also more easily renewed than the plantings of beds and borders.

Containers need to be in scale with their surroundings. This large, handsome pot provides the focus of attention for the terraced area. It would be satisfactory, even if not planted.

***Tulipa* 'Madame Lefeber'** Tulips grow well in pots for a season, making a good display in spring, especially when given a background emphasizing their colour.

Containers can be used to decorate steps, larger free-standing pots at the bottom and smaller ones on the steps. Use drought-resistant plants so the steps are not always wet. Scented plants are pleasant to brush past.

Planting *a* Container

Do not leave air pockets around the plant's roots – they do not grow well in air.

Repot before winter, so that the plant is growing strongly before the cold weather.

Shade for a few days after repotting in hot weather, to give the plant time to re-establish.

1. The base of a clay pot will require 'crocking' – pieces of broken pot put in to cover the drainage hole(s) and prevent soil loss. The holes in plastic pots are generally smaller and do not need crocks.

2. Choose a pot larger, but not too much so, than the root ball. Scrape some of the old top layer of compost off the root ball and carefully tease out some roots.

3. Next choose the appropriate compost for your plant, lime-free, or quick-draining, or with added water-retaining granules.

4. Part fill the pot, leaving room for the root ball. Fill round the plant, nearly to the rim, firming carefully.

Potting On

Plants will suffer in pots if they outgrow them. Replant perennials in fresh compost in a larger container. They can alternatively be divided or you can trim the roots of shrubby forms by about a quarter.

PLANTING *a* CONTAINER

PLANT YOUR BULBS IN AUTUMN for spring flowering. If your winters are very cold, store the containers in a shed or garage, or protect with sacking or bubble polythene. Many bulbs will rot if frozen solid and the soil in pots is much more vulnerable to freezing than in the open ground.

Spring Pots. The variegated ivy stands out brightly against the hedge, the tulips and primrose adding a welcome splash of colour.

◆ *The effectiveness of the group is increased by the differing heights of the pots.*

PLANTS *for* SUN

ANNUALS AND SOFT PERENNIALS provide many of the plants suitable for pots on sunny patios. If a lot are required this can be an expensive enterprise. Seeds can be germinated on well-lit window-sills and grown on in small frames outside. Cuttings from perennials can be overwintered on window-sills and rapidly grow to good-sized plants in a frame or greenhouse.

***Rosa* 'Sweet Dream'** Patio roses need a fertile soil, sun, good drainage, deadheading and a light pruning in spring. 20 × 30cm/8in × 1ft

◆ *Roses do best without other plants growing through them.*

Schizanthus Attractive annuals with variously coloured flowers. May need some support. Pinch the growing tips of young plants to encourage bushiness.
60 × 30cm/2 × 1ft

Containers carefully chosen, grouped together and packed with plants, make a spectacular display. The colour of the silver **helichrysum** and pale blue **lobelia** complement each other and set off the shocking pink **pelargonium**. The blue ***Convolvulus sabatius*** shows up well with the glistening white **marguerite**. Trailing plants help to bind the design together.

PLANTS *for* SUN

PLANTS GROWN IN POTS WILL NEED REGULAR FEEDING if they are to give a good display throughout the summer. A liquid feed high in potash is required for flower production and nitrogen for foliage. During the flowering season it is sensible to feed plants at least once a week.

***Brugmansia* (Angel's trumpet, Datura)** Fragrant. Tender. Water well. 2 × 2.4m/6 × 8ft

◆ *Daturas are poisonous, especially the flowers and fruit. Handle with care.*

***Heliotropium* × *hybridum* (Cherry pie)** Corymbs of scented flowers all summer. Not hardy. 30 × 45cm/1 × 1½ft

***Felicia amelloides* (Blue marguerite)** Not hardy, so collect seeds or take cuttings. 45 × 30cm/1½ × 1ft

***Agave americana* (Century plant)** Succulent with sword leaves, tipped with spines. Dangerous to children. Not hardy. 1 × 1m/3 × 3ft

Plumbago capensis A beautiful container shrub, flowering all summer, but needs to be frost free. 1.5m × 60cm/5 × 2ft

PLANTS *for* SUN

Argyranthemum White, pink or yellow double or single flowers. Dead-head regularly. Tender. 60 × 45cm/2 × 1½ft

Abutilon* × *hybridum Makes a splendid pot plant but needs to winter frost-free. Prune in early spring. 1m × 60cm/3 × 2ft

***Callistemon rigidus* (Bottle brush)** Will need some frost protection in all but the mildest areas. 1 × 1.2m/3 × 4ft

Begonia Pendulous begonias, trained as standards, make very effective pot plants. 60cm × 1m/2 × 3ft

Echeveria Makes an interesting container plant for the patio or terrace. Needs little water. Not hardy. 7.5 × 15cm/3 × 6in

Gazania These daisy flowers open and close with the sun. 23 × 23cm/9 × 9in

***Narcissus* 'Tête à Tête'** One of the best multi-headed dwarf daffodils. Feed in spring and repot each summer. 23cm/9in

The violas, if the winter is not too hard, will brighten this display until the tulips flower.

***Lilium* 'Connecticut King'** Lilies grow well in pots. Use good compost and plant deeply. 75cm/2½ft tall

The modern varieties of **Regal pelargoniums** are very free-flowering, especially if fed and dead-headed regularly. 60 × 30cm/2 × 1ft

Most plants in pots – not succulents – need watering once a day in summer, twice if very hot.

It is better to water early or late, rather than when the sun is hottest.

Water-retaining granules can be mixed with the compost at planting to reduce drying out.

PLANTS *for* PART SHADE

IT IS IMPORTANT TO CHOOSE PLANTS FOR SHADE that are adapted, like woodlanders, to live in low-light conditions. Those preferring sun will grow lank, with pale leaves and few flowers, if grown in shade.

There are many varieties of **Hosta**, from large plants, suitable for a barrel, to plants for a small pot. Silver or gold variegations look good in the shade.

◆ *Watch out for slugs in the early spring when the leaves are unfurling.*

***Hydrangea macrophylla* 'Madame Emile Mouillère'**
A beautiful, but tender, hydrangea with large white flowers which become tinted pink later in the season. Needs semi-shade and a moist soil. 1.2 × 2m/4 × 6ft

***Rhododendron flavidum* 'Album'** Small rhododendron suitable for pot culture. Prune after flowering. E, 60cm × 1m/ 2 × 3ft

◆ *Rhododendrons need a lime-free compost and must not dry out.*

Primula obconica Pink, red-purple or blue-purple flowers in early spring. Usually grown as an annual. The light green leaves are hairy and cause an allergic reaction in some people's skins. 45 × 20cm/ 1½ft × 8in

Euonymus fortunei Makes an effective standard. E, 4.5 × 1.5m/15 × 5ft unpruned

◆ *There are many variegated varieties available.*

PLANTS *for* PART SHADE

***Begonia semperflorens* 'Kalinka Rose'** Tuberous begonias are very versatile and will grow in sun or semi-shade.
60cm × 1m/2 × 3ft

Pieris japonica Evergreen shrub, with red young shoots and racemes of white flowers in spring.
E, 3 × 3m/10 × 10ft

◆ *Pieris needs a lime-free soil and must not dry out.*

***Hosta* 'Halcyon'** Blue textured leaves and lilac flowers in midsummer.
60 × 60cm/2 × 2ft

Eucomis bicolor (Pineapple plant) A spectacular bulb with long-lasting flowers in midsummer and attractive seed capsules. 45cm/1½ft

***Polystichum setiferum* 'Acutilobum'** (Soft shield fern) The attractive fronds retain their colour all winter. 1 × 1m/3 × 3ft

Lilium regale Beautiful fragrant summer-flowering lily. Stem rooting, so plant deeply. 1.2–2m/4–6ft tall

***Lilium* 'Pink Perfection'** A tall hybrid of *L. regale* which bears large scented trumpets. 1.2m/4ft or more

PLANTS *for* PART SHADE

PLANTS IN POTS IN SEMI-SHADE do not need as much water as those in full sun, but more care is needed removing dead flowers and foliage to prevent the spread of moulds and other diseases.

Acer palmatum dissectum Beautiful cut leaves and superb autumn colour. 4.5 × 2.4m/15 × 8ft eventually

◆ *These deciduous trees need protection from wind and sun.*

***Cassiope* 'Muirhead'** Dwarf heath-like shrub with white bell flowers in spring. For lime-free soil. E, 10 × 30cm/4 × 12in

***Tradescantia virginiana* 'Purple Dome'** A hardy plant, flowering from early summer to autumn. 60 × 45cm/2 × 1½ft

Magnificent specimens of ***Fuchsia* 'Checkerboard'** and ***F.* 'Orange Mirage'** raised on a plinth.

◆ *A high-phosphate feed in summer helps flowering.*

TUBS *and* BARRELS

MOST TUBS AND BARRELS used in the garden are wooden. These should be treated on the inside so that the wood does not rot, either with a preserving fluid or by briefly burning the inside of the barrel to produce a thin protective layer of charcoal.

***Trachycarpus fortunei* (Chusan palm)** Needs shelter from cold winds. E, 2–3m/6–10ft high

◆ *Pot up offsets to make new plants.*

This copper tub makes a splendid centrepiece to this circle of roof tiles and granite sets.

◆ *The apricot red and yellow shades tone well with the blue-green of the copper.*

Ivy-leaved pelargoniums achieve great height, when carefully staked, and flower all summer. The silver helichrysum cools the pink very effectively.

◆ *This barrel is well framed by the dark green background.*

TUBS *and* BARRELS

Evergreens including a box ball around a summer planting of marguerites.

***Camellia* 'Anticipation'** Camellias make excellent shrubs for a large container of the acid, humus-rich soil they relish. With the aid of rollers, the barrel may be moved from its prominent flowering position and placed so that it retreats into the background for the rest of the year.

SINKS *and* TROUGHS

To minimise back strain, put your trough in its final position before filling it with compost.

Keep your trough off the ground with bricks or slate for good drainage.

New troughs 'age' better in the shade.

A combination of troughs and pots makes an attractive group in the corner of a patio. The pots can be changed to prolong the flowering season.

◆ *This is a good way to combine plants with different growing requirements.*

Before filling the trough with compost, cover the drainage holes with crocks.

Top dress the compost with gravel to keep the plants' necks dry to help prevent rotting.

This handsome stone trough makes a good home for alpine sedums.

◆ *Complementary plantings beneath unite the trough with its surroundings.*

This attractive trough of pansies and lobelia will give a long display if fed and dead-headed.

◆ *In front, both flowers and seed-heads are beautiful.*

Sinks *and* Troughs

Sinks and troughs are most commonly used for small alpine plants. Attractive, semi-permanent miniature gardens can be created in this way, but narrow troughs can also be planted like window boxes, the display changing with the seasons.

The trough shown opposite is used here for a splendid spring effect. Again the planting has been kept unfussy and simple, just two: grape hyacinths (muscari) and double daisies (*Bellis perennis*).

◆ *The spires of the muscari contrast well with the saucer-flowers of the daisies.*

SINKS *and* TROUGHS

Stone trough on legs with white petunias rising above blue lobelia.

Another elegant trough with nemesias making a brilliant display.

Trailing silver helichrysum, pelargoniums and fuchsias in another raised trough.

Lewisia cotyledon hybrids flowering in a stone alpine trough in summer.

◆ *Lewisias are best kept in an alpine house in winter to prevent rot from wet; or outside, grow them on their sides in a wall.*

Foliage plants (begonias and fern) with the hardy annual hare's tail grass (*Lagurus ovatus*). An original planting.

Beautiful old trough with sempervivums and a little bush of *Alyssum spinosum roseum*.

Hypertufa

Stone troughs are increasingly rare and also expensive. An alternative is to make a hypertufa trough. Hypertufa is a very versatile material and can look good quite quickly. When aged it can be hard to distinguish from stone.

Safety

Take care not to get concrete products into your eyes and on the skin. Wear goggles and gloves. Wash well when the job is complete.

1. Hypertufa is made from one part each of cement, dry sharp, or concreting, sand and finely sieved peat or coco fibre. PVA bonding agent will give strength and flowability. Mix and add water, mixing until the compound just flows.

2. Find two boxes to give walls 4–5cm/1½–2in thick. Put the base layer in the larger box and make two drainage holes. Tamp. Place the second box centrally on the base. Larger troughs need wire reinforcement for the base and sides.

3. Support the sides of the outer box and fill the inner box with sand, then continue filling the sides. Tamp. Cover with wet fabric and leave for 36 hours. Carefully remove fabric and boxes.

4. Shape with old knives and a stiff brush. Open up drain holes. Replace wet fabric and leave to set for 2 or 3 days, when it will be strong enough to move. Plant one week later.

Unusual Containers

This elegant lead urn, and the granite sets surrounding it, would flatter any planting.

Home-made Water Garden. A wooden container with a liner makes an attractively planted water garden.

These chimney pots make an interesting group with the wall pots. They also look good with hanging plants.

A large glazed jar with its agave, and the trellis work, gives an exotic air to a patio.

These alpines and dwarf conifers are growing very happily in this old iron bath and make a very satisfying group with the iron pot spilling its red rock rose onto the gravel.

◆ *The imaginative placing of the iron pot distinguishes this grouping.*

UNUSUAL CONTAINERS

A PLANT-CONTAINER CAN BE ANYTHING that holds compost from a plastic ice-cream tub to a lead cistern. All that is required is some growing medium and drainage holes. Pots can be painted, or clad in wood for effect.

This barrow, with its load of startling white marguerites (argyranthemums), dangling pink pelargoniums and blue lobelia, is cleverly placed in front of a yew hedge which provides an ideal background.

◆ *Many artefacts can be put to decorative use in the garden.*

A painted barrow is given its own cobbled area to form a novel focal point in the garden.

Forest trees can be grown in small containers, if carefully watered and pruned. Their branches may be wired to achieve the desired shape.

There are still old washhouse coppers in rural areas which can be put to good use as planters, preferably with drainage holes in the base.

HANGING BASKETS

HANGING BASKETS PROVIDE additional space for plants, add height to your displays and can be placed at different levels to enliven a boring wall. They can be hung on any strong structure to make a display in the middle of your patio.

The bright colours in this basket are beautifully set off by the grey stone wall.

◆ *The trailing variegated glechoma (ground ivy) links the basket to the window box.*

Hanging baskets are ideal for trailing plants, like **ivy-leaved pelargoniums** and **lobelia** which form great cascades, while **petunias** and **impatiens** (busy lizzies) add bulk. These will make a colourful display all summer if well fed, watered and dead-headed.

These twin baskets benefit from lots of blue to make a contrast to the red bricks.

◆ *Silver foliage also looks good against bricks.*

Planting *a* Basket

Moisture Granules

Watering is a big problem with hanging baskets, but these granules will help if they are added to the planting compost when you make up the basket.

The picture below shows the same granules twenty minutes after water has been added to them. They have absorbed it and the basket will enjoy damp conditions as the granules gradually release their moisture.

If your basket does dry out, get it down and stand it in water for a couple of hours.

Choose as large a basket as the situation allows; larger baskets dry out less quickly than smaller ones. A liner is required to hold in the planting compost and moisture. There are various types available, including the traditional sphagnum moss, but here we show how to plant up a basket using a simple polythene liner.

1. The aim is to plant the basket sufficiently densely that the liner is not visible, just a complete sphere of flowers. Before filling the basket with soil, cut holes in the liner around the sides. **2.** Gradually fill the basket with planting compost, moisture granules and fertilizer (if this is not already present in the compost), putting plants through the holes you have made as the basket fills up.

3. Cut off any spare liner. Squeeze in a good number of plants to produce a well covered basket and then water thoroughly. It will take three or four weeks for the plants to develop sufficiently to cover the basket. During this time it may be best to keep the basket in an easily accessible, sheltered place for watering before hanging it in its final location.

PLANTING *a* BASKET

Your basket will do best in a position sheltered from wind. It will need a strong bracket, firmly fixed.

For ease of maintenance and watering, pulleys are available to enable the basket to be lowered.

In dry, hot weather your basket will need watering twice a day. Automatic watering systems are available.

If the basket looks tired in midsummer use a high nitrogen liquid feed for a fortnight.

SITING HANGING BASKETS

HANGING BASKETS will look best in sheltered positions as wind causes them to dry out quickly and breaks brittle foliage. If they are placed too high, watering can be a problem. Their main function is as decoration and they should be sited where they can be seen to best advantage.

Baskets hanging from a pergola, a covered terrace and at the entrance to a house – three positions where they will be best appreciated.

◆ *Scented plants would be particularly successful on a pergola.*

Plants *for* Baskets

Plants for hanging baskets need to be tough to survive in their exposed environment. Trailing plants and those which produce a mass of blooms on short stems to cover the basket with foliage and flowers are a better choice than those with tall rigid stems.

Helichrysum petiolare An indispensable plant for hanging baskets. The cool silver foliage sets off bright colours and hangs gracefully.

Ivies do well in semi-shade or in a winter display and trail daintily.

A much rounder effect is gained by using only one type of plant. In a mild winter, these pansies will flower until spring.

◆ *Even in winter, water will be required, especially in cold windy weather.*

PLANTS *for* BASKETS

Consider the background before choosing the plants.

Petunias in their various shades make a bold splash. Modern varieties are more rain resistant.

This combination of perlargoniums (geraniums), petunias, calceolarias and impatiens (busy lizzies) makes a colourful display.

Diascia vigilis This hardy diascia will grow happily in a hanging basket and, with a little trimming, will look good all summer.

***Fuchsia* 'Miss California'** Trailing fuchsias show themselves to advantage in hanging baskets.

◆ *Fuchsias do well in shade or partial shade.*

Lotus berthelotii This spectacular silver-leaved plant enjoys sun and adds drama to any hanging basket.

Blue lobelia is a very useful foil to reds and pinks, cooling strident shades. Easily raised from seed.

PLANTS *for* BASKETS

Use baskets with saucers where drips could be a nuisance.

Bidens ferulifolia has bright yellow daisy flowers which flow over the edges of baskets.

Mimulus (Monkey flower) comes in many shades of red, orange and yellow, sometimes with spots.

Calceolaria prefers a light acid soil in sun or partial shade.

Some varieties of patio and ground-cover roses can be grown for a short period in the basket.

Begonia semperflorens
Always a tidy plant with red or green foliage and red, pink or white flowers.

◆ *They grow happily in sun or shade.*

***Impatiens* 'Picotee Swirl'**
This busy lizzie would brighten any shady corner in summer.

◆ *A basket with one variety can look very effective.*

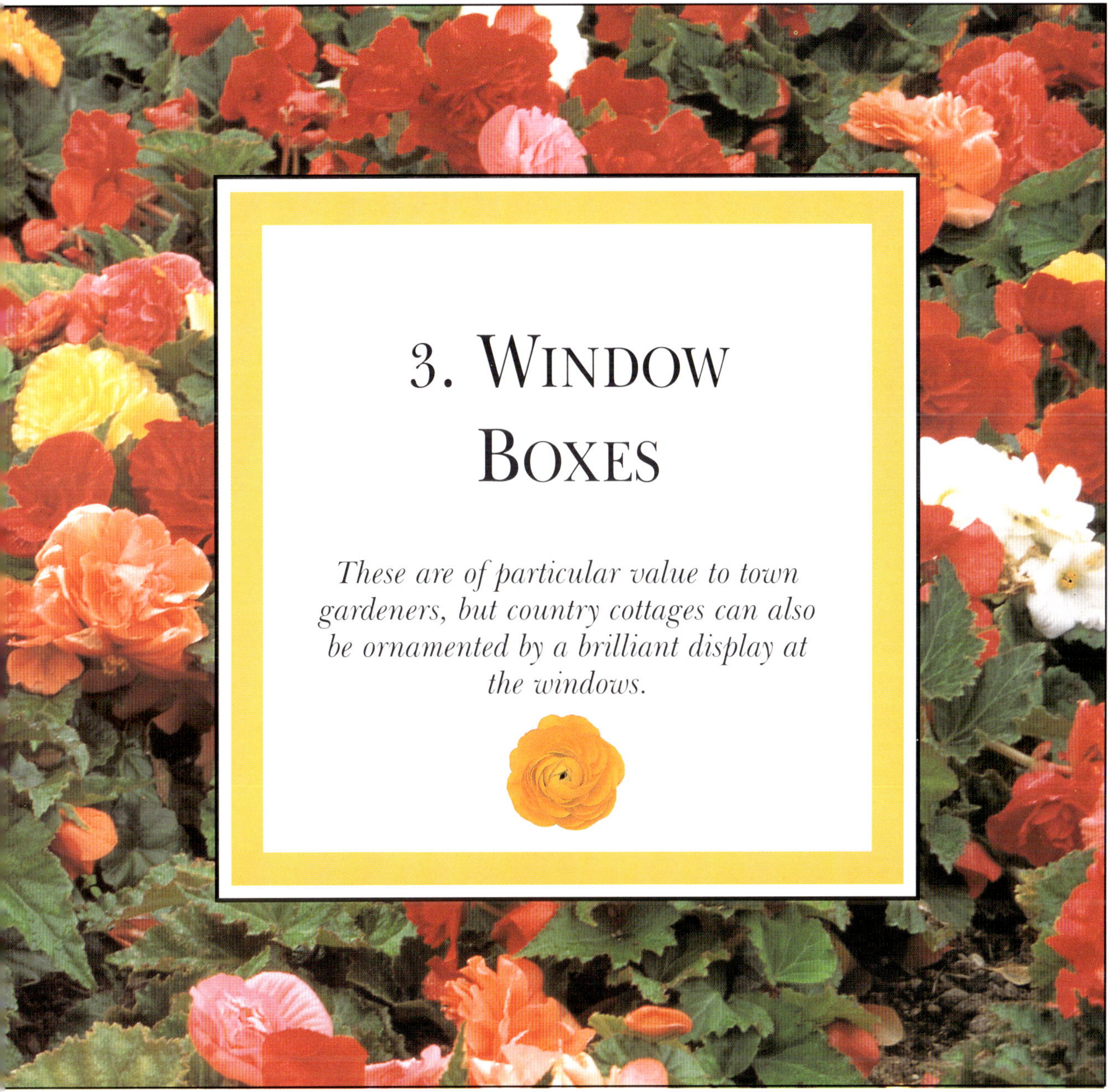

3. Window Boxes

These are of particular value to town gardeners, but country cottages can also be ornamented by a brilliant display at the windows.

Window Box Systems

This raised bed, made from bricks, makes a good window box, providing a cool root run and needing less watering than a conventional box.

Check window sills for weight bearing capacity.

Water gently to avoid washing compost onto walls and windows below.

Before buying a window box, check how your windows open!

This window box, with a plastic insert, works well as the wood will rot less quickly, not being in contact with the soil, and the display can be changed easily, when required.

◆ *This system also allows you to dunk the trough in water if it dries out.*

Plastic boxes need little maintenance and are light – an advantage on weak sills.

A hay rack with a liner can look very attractive where sills are narrow.

These wooden boxes, with decorative restraining bars, blend well with the austere window surrounds.

Window Box Systems

Try to choose a simple window box in style with your building – a hay rack may look out of place on a modern block, or too ornate a box may dominate your plants. Above all, whatever you choose must be secure and able to bear the weight of soil and plants.

A simple restraining bar can be very effective, allowing the use of plants in pots which can be changed through the seasons to maintain the display.

◆ *Take care that top-heavy plants cannot fall over the bar.*

A Spring Display

Winter displays of pansies and evergreens can easily be changed to spring displays with the help of daffodils, tulips or hyacinths to give extra colour and stronger shapes and to contrast with the existing plants.

This combination of clipped boxes, ivies and skimmias will have provided interest all winter and the scented flowers of the skimmias now herald spring.

These rich violet pansies and glowing yellow tulips would brighten any dull spring day.

◆ *Fewer colours often make a greater impact.*

The daffodils provide a link between the hay rack and the small bed, extending the colour across the whole elevation.

Compact wallflowers can add scent as well as colour.

Bulbs grown in pots are useful for filling gaps.

The modern varieties of winter pansies have a long flowering season and, in mild winters, flower straight through, with the best flush in the spring.

◆ *Dead-head regularly and check for greenfly in the spring.*

This display is essentially short term, but magnificent while it lasts and is suitable for boxes with interchangeable liners. The **trailing ivy** clothes the box and balances the height of the **tulips** and **hyacinths**. The tulips' strong shape cuts through the frothy blue **forget-me-nots** while the hyacinths' rich fragrance can drift into the house through an open window.

Summer Blooms

Now is the time for extravagant growth and vibrant colours. A little planning will give a dramatic display which, with a little maintenance (feeding, dead-heading and watering), will last well into autumn.

The shocking pink petunias, red ivy-leaved pelargoniums (geraniums) combined with the dashing orange shades of the nemesia and cooled by the dark blue white-eyed lobelia, make a stunning display.

◆ *The white walls and curtains make a perfect cool background.*

Summer Blooms

The large variety of plants in this window box, with strongly differing shapes and colours, accentuates the vertical line of the split blinds behind.

◆ *This sort of effect can also be achieved by using separate pots.*

The ivy on the wall surrounding this window box, with its pelargoniums (geraniums) and petunias, gives a charming cottagey effect, as if it all grew out of the wall unaided.

◆ *The ivy may be kept in bounds by pruning.*

This window box of begonias, petunias, dahlia, impatiens and lobelia adds height to the collection of plants beneath. The use of similar colours unifies the container.

◆ *Reds look well against subdued backgrounds.*

***Pelargonium* 'Roller's Pioneer'** Ivy-leaved pelargoniums are excellent in containers, having succulent, drought-resistant leaves. They will flower in cascades until the frosts, or all winter in warmth.

Use plants with similar food and water requirements together to ease maintenance.

When you buy plants, choose the sturdier young plants showing buds rather than those that are lanky and flowering.

Always plant something scented in your displays.

Summer Blooms

Watering is best done in the cool of the evening, to reduce evaporation loss.

Gazania Sun-loving cream and yellow flowers well set off by bright silver foliage.

Petunia These are well suited to a sunny position but are less happy in a rainy season. A mainstay of most window boxes.

The petunias, verbena and pelargoniums, plants with similar requirements, combine very well to give a good display.

The zonal pelargoniums are well matched with the petunias, falling forwards and flowing into the variegated ground ivy, carrying the colour down the wall.

Zonal pelargoniums are strongly growing, upright plants and can make a fine display on their own.

SUMMER BLOOMS

Never give liquid feeds to a dry container.

Pelargoniums are commonly called geraniums.

The white fuchsia and the apricot and yellow argyranthemums (marguerites) are highlighted by the bright blue lobelia, creating a lovely effect against the warm brick wall.

A display of trailing pelargoniums giving continuous colour and good, disease-resistant foliage.

Impatiens (busy lizzies) have a tidy habit, flower continuously and are happy in shade.

Tuberous begonias are available in many colours and, with their shining foliage, give a tropical air.

The pendulous begonias add a luxuriant feel with their shiny pointed leaves and lush satiny flowers glowing against the blue-mauve of the zonal pelargonium.

AUTUMN *and* WINTER

UNLESS YOU LIVE IN A FROST-FREE ZONE, most of your summer and autumn plants will be dead by mid-winter, but it is not necessary for your window box to be full of depressing flowerless sticks all winter. There are many hardy evergreens which will brighten this season, with a minimum of maintenance, some of which will then come into flower in spring.

The variegated hebe is balanced by the ivy, the gold and cream set off by the black window box.

◆ *Check that the compost is not too dry at regular intervals.*

The griselinia adds height and substance to this arrangement.

◆ *These shrubs can be kept for several winters.*

This is an effective arrangement of silver and gold foliage with the splash of red berries.

◆ *An occasional trim will keep the little shrubs smart.*

This combination of evergreens makes a satisfying display. The **heathers** will flower in late winter and set off the clipped **boxes** which give shape and height. The **ivies** trail, softening the edges and countering the rigid shapes of the boxes and heathers. Some summer-flowering heathers change colour in winter to bright reds and golds and can therefore be valuable for their winter foliage.